The Millionaire's Secret

A Handbook For Building Wealth In Tough Times

Ron Taylor

iUniverse, Inc.

New York   Bloomington

The Millionaire's Secret
A Handbook For Building Wealth In Tough Times

iUniverse books may be ordered through booksellers or by contacting:

iUniverse
1663 Liberty Drive
Bloomington, IN 47403
www.iuniverse.com
1-800-Authors (1-800-288-4677)

Because of the dynamic nature of the Internet, any Web addresses or links contained in this book may have changed since publication and may no longer be valid.

ISBN: 978-1-4502-0723-2 (sc)
ISBN: 978-1-4502-0724-9 (ebk)

Printed in the United States of America

iUniverse rev. date: 1/7/2010

"Pursue your dreams with passion, and let no obstacle deter your progress."

The Millionaire's Secret

To My Team Partners,

The phenomenal success of the Millionaire's Secret wealth building strategies discussed in this book can be attributed to the teamwork and feedback I have received from my business partners located around the world.

Together, we have made a difference.

Table of Contents

Introduction
Wealth in America

If you are either broke, or not making as much money as you want, welcome to the party. I wrote this book for you.

We live in the richest nation the world has ever known. Yet, less than 5% of the retirees in this country are independently wealthy, and the vast majority of us depend upon Social Security and handouts just to get by.

Something is wrong with that picture, and the odds suggest that you cannot achieve financial freedom.

But, I'm betting you do not consider yourself a statistic.

In my opinion, if you are willing to learn the basic principles of creating wealth, and will apply this knowledge in a concerted and deliberate manner, you can achieve wealth.

Achieving wealth in America is not about how much you earn, but how wisely you use what you earn. This book is aimed at helping you to both increase your income, and manage your money properly.

Among other things, you will learn that spending more than you earn in an effort to impress friends and neighbors with your material possessions is a recipe for financial disaster. Additionally, lacking the patience to invest for the long-term, develop action oriented goal statements, and failing to protect yourself with proper insurance and legal advice, are all indicators of poor financial management.

Again, it's not what you earn, but what you do with it that matters.

When it comes to wealth building and any business endeavor, one of the biggest obstacles you will encounter is the programming of your parents, friends, school, and media. Popular opinion has taught us that wealth and success comes to those who are lucky, or cheats.

I hope the following principles will help you realize this is not true.

Measuring Your Wealth

One standard measurement of wealth is a six-figure income, which pertains to the number of digits in your annual income. A six-figure income equals anything above $100,000.

The most recent data from the Internal Revenue Service, 2007 tax returns, show exactly where your current income places you relative to other taxpayers. According to the IRS, an income of $32,000 puts you in the top 50 percentile, and an income of over $66,000 places you in the top 25 percentile. To reach that magical top 10% of all earners requires an annual income of at least $113,000.

According to the U.S. Census Bureau, in 2004, the number of households with income between $100,000 and $149,999 exceeded 11 million, 3.5 million American households had income between $150,000 and $199,999, 1.3 million households had incomes between $200,000 and $249,999, and 1.7 million households had income above $250,000 per year.

Unfortunately, the wealth of America cannot simply be measured by income.

According to an article written by David Francis and published in the May 23, 2005 edition of *Christian Science Monitor,* nearly 20% of American households have either zero net worth, or actually owe more than they are worth.

Furthermore, according to Francis, 25% of American households do not have sufficient cash reserves or other assets to support themselves above the poverty level for three months, and 33% of households do not even have an active bank account.

What ever happened to the land of opportunity? Americans are killing themselves with uncontrolled spending, easy credit, and a complete lack of budgeting or saving skills.

Finding Your Wealth Quotient

So how does one measure wealth? And, when does a person know if he or she has achieved "wealth?"

For the purposes of this book, wealth is defined as an income level derived from passive sources that allows you to live without depending upon a job.

This emphasis on "passive income" is a critically important millionaire secret.

Passive sources are any income source that throws off a positive cash flow, that you can bank or spend. For example, the cash left over from a rental property after all expenses are paid, is passive income. Likewise, interest from a certificate of deposit, or dividends from stock investments, are examples of passive income.

With this definition in mind, the key to creating wealth is to figure out how to create and build passive income sources.

To measure my progress in this area, I use a simple formula:

Passive Income Divided By Total Living Expenses Equals Your Wealth Quotient

Consider this example: If you had $1,200 per month in combined passive income from a real estate investment and your cash savings account, and $4,500 in monthly expenses to survive (house payment, household expenses, etc), your wealth quotient equals:

1,200/4,500 = .26

The ideal is to achieve a quotient of 1 or greater. The number .26 represents approximately one quarter of your desired quotient of 1 or greater. Change the numbers and watch what happens:

$$3{,}000/4{,}500 = .66$$

$$4{,}500/4{,}500 = 1$$

$$6{,}000/4{,}500 = 1.33$$

The key to long term financial success is to build passive income, and free yourself from the need to work or "earn" a living. In my opinion, when your wealth quotient reaches 1, you have achieved wealth.

The rest is simply a matter of how much margin for safety and extra luxuries you wish to obtain.

Creating Wealth With Passive Income

Keep in mind that passive and portfolio income is typically earned from fully insured and maintained real estate that provides a positive cash flow, interest from savings, dividends from Blue Chip stocks and bonds, and royalties from books, patents, and music you may own the rights to.

These rights to intellectual property, combined with the equity in real estate owned and various certificates of deposit, stocks, and bonds, comprises what is known as your capital base.

As your capital base grows, you are able to generate greater amounts of passive and portfolio income (PPI). When your PPI exceeds your basic living expenses, you have achieved a level of wealth that enables you to make riskier investments in the pursuit of higher yields and return on investment (ROI).

The key here, which is a lesson I learned from both "The Richest Man in Babylon" and the school of hardknocks, is not to erode your capital base by making risky investments or spending the money that makes up the foundation to your wealth building aspirations.

As my rough sketches illustrate, you should use only the cash proceeds that are above and beyond your basic living expenses (derived from your capital base) to make wealth building investments and/or purchase the goodies in life.

If you violate this rule and consistently dip into your capital base, you will need to keep your day job to feed your consumption habits.

I am not in any way advocating a Spartan lifestyle — after all, the pursuit of wealth is only worthwhile if you are allowed to enjoy a higher quality of life for yourself and your family.

Creating Wealth With Delayed Gratification

The basic tenet of this book is that you should carefully manage your money to ensure your investment and wealth building goals are heading in the right direction. In the short term this may mean cutting back on the niceties, but the rewards later on will allow you to enjoy the good things in life above and beyond the norm.

Robert Allen makes this point perfectly clear in his book, "Nothing Down," where he compares your pursuit of wealth to a rocket ship leaving earth towards space. In the early stages, just after liftoff, your progress is slow and awkward, but as you gain experience and continue to build your capital base, your rocketship gains speed until it begins to break free of the earth's gravitational pull.

Allen's analogy is a great lesson in wealth building and is well worth reading.

Again, this concept of building passive income to create wealth is vitally important to your acquisition of wealth. Follow the steps of creating multiple streams of income that ideally throw off positive cashflow to your hip pocket with minimal effort.

The Millionaire's Secret In A Nutshell:

- Create multiple streams of income from passive sources.
- Use this positve cashflow to offset your living expenses.
- Use the excess (passive income above and beyond your living expenses) to feed your investment activities.
- When your wealth quotient exceeds 1, you have achieved a moderate level of wealth.

The "Income" Route To Wealth

Another definition of wealth considers income, where an annual income equal to or greater than 1 million dollars constitutes wealth.

Using the net worth criteria alone, 3% of American households qualify as "wealthy," and according to recent studies of millionaires in America, most millionaires (million dollar net worth) live by modest means, drive non-luxury cars, and do not own luxury homes.

Based on the "income" definition of wealth, wealthy Americans are generally professionals such as attorneys, surgeons, and scientists, with the entrepreneurial group gaining ground. A great book to read on this subject is *The Millionaire Next Door*, by Thomas J. Stanley and William D. Danko.

Prior to the real estate and economic meltdown of 2008 and 2009, various consumer watch groups and the U.S. Census Bureau estimated there were over 8 million millionaire households in the United States, much of which was realized through high home values.

Sadly, the recent turn of events in our economy demands an alternative means of defining wealth in America.

Rich Dad's Definition Of Wealth

Robert Kiyosaki does not allow the inclusion of personal residences in his calculations of net worth in his *Rich Dad, Poor Dad* book series, and prefers to limit such calculations to investment property, liquid assets, and businesses owned or controlled.

Using his definiiton of wealth, the number of millionaire status households in America would be significantly lower.

In November 2007, author and financial wealth expert Russ Alan Prince estimated there were 8.4 million American households with net worth's from 1-10 million dollars. A number he claims is growing at around 15% per year.

And despite the recent housing market turmoil and massive layoffs by Fortune 500 companies, Americans continue to find ways to create wealth.

One example of outrageous success is Ashley Qualls' creation of the website www.whateverlife.com, reported in a Yahoo news article published 31 October 2007.

According to the article, Ashley generates over $1 million per year in revenue selling custom designed MySpace profiles. Interestingly, Ashley is a 17-year-old high school dropout.

Ashley's success is certainly not the norm, but it does serve to illustrate that opportunity to create wealth is not dead — in fact, it seems to be getting better and better.

It is my hope that you will think of the current economic turmoil as a challenge and not an insurmountable barrier. Learn the basics of creating wealth discussed in this book, and then take massive action to make something positive happen for yourself.

Creating Wealth Warren Buffett Style

Warren Buffett once stated, "It is easier to *create* money than it is to spend it."

The operative word in this statement is his use of the word "create." By "create," Buffett does not mean to make or earn money. Creating wealth is not about getting a second job or negotiating a pay raise, although these things can certainly help in the beginning stages of wealth building.

Creating wealth is about finding ways to preserve the money you do earn, putting it to proper use, and learning how to develop income sources from outside your normal day job, as discussed in the Introduction above.

Warren Buffett created his billion-dollar empire by investing in companies and adding value to their product or service. As a beginning wealth builder you can similarly add value to the enterprises you undertake by producing a better product, marketing your services more effectively, and making wise investments in real estate, stocks, bonds, and intellectual properties.

Another quote from Warren Buffett illustrates his philosophy towards investing. Buffet states: "I don't try to jump over 7-foot bars: I look around for 1-foot bars that I can step over."

This is an interesting strategy that you will see over and over in creating wealth and investment success type books.

Essentially, Buffett is telling you not to overwhelm yourself with the need to hit a homerun every time you step up to bat. A steady stream of singles wins games. From an investment or business startup perspective, this means you don't have to bet the entire farm on one deal, nor do you have to make a million on your next stock market investment.

This philosophy is echoed throughout this book, where I implore you to think big, but to also think in terms of small successes repeated over and over. Again, if you can make a hundred bucks doing something within your current capabilities and resources, could you repeat it?

Creating wealth can be that simple.

Donald Trump And The Numbers Game

Donald Trump is an excellent example of this numbers game. While he came from a long line of successful entrepreneurs, Trump can be considered a self-made billionaire.

In his book "Think Like a Billionaire," Trump outlines his strategy for success. One of his key points that most self-made men and women can relate to is the need to go it alone.

Aside from the investor and lender support you will need along the way (which you will pay for in the form of interest and dividends), the process of creating personal wealth is a solitary one. Nobody cares about your finances quite as much as you. Nobody will hand you an empire. And nobody will sell you a thriving business.

Creating personal wealth is up to you.

It's up to you to take a lump of clay, known as an idea, and shape it into something valuable.

Fortunately, we live in a society that rewards ingenuity, hard work, and perseverance. Use the millionaire secrets in this book to educate yourself and start the potter's wheel turning in your direction.

A Little Disclaimer

In terms of a disclaimer, I should mention that I am not a licensed stockbroker, attorney, or certified financial planner. The information in this book is based purely on my personal experience and opinion. Please conduct due diligence in all of your financial and business decisions.

"Don't chase success. Rather, focus your thoughts and efforts on doing what needs to be done, today.

In the end, success and happiness will find you."

The Millionaire's Secret

Millionaire Secret #1
Spend Less Than You Earn

The first step in the wealth building process is the most difficult.

Spending less than you earn is an obstacle to success, and in my experience, trashes the dreams of more wealth builders than anything else.

Quite simply, if you cannot control your spending habits, you do not have the potential to achieve wealth — short of winning the lottery, landing a mega-millions sports contract, or inventing a cure for cancer.

Here's the challenge I'm laying down for you: Learn to spend less than you earn by either decreasing your expenditures or increasing your income.

Stop Wasting Your Hard Earned Money

Try not to focus on cutting out all the good things in your life or forcing a draconian budget on your family. Instead, cut out the obvious wasting of money, stop buying frivolous things on credit, and figure out how to make $300 to $500 extra each month, outside your current job.

Please don't think in terms of another part time job.

Think in terms of what home-based business or investment can bring in the money.

At a minimum, you should strive to spend less than 90% of your after tax income, while ideally this number should be closer to 70%.

Use the remaining 10-30% of your after tax income to build your savings account, and establish a cash reserve equal to at least six months worth of your living expenses.

Ironically, by spending less than you earn you dramatically alter the wealth quotient, as discussed in the Introduction. Technically, you have become wealthy when you can live off less than you earn. However, this is not good enough for me, and I doubt you or your family will find it acceptable either.

Putting Your Wealth Goals Into Perspective

National statistics on housing and the cost of living can help put your expenses into perspective. According to the Bureau of Labor Statistics (BLS), the average employed adult in America earns $36,764.

At least 17% of that will be consumed by income and Social Security taxes, leaving about $30,500 in expendable income, or about $2,500 per month. As renters, the median gross rent is $602 per month, and as homeowners the median costs are $1,088.

Homeowners in America use around 21.7% of their income for housing, and while homeowners without mortgages represent up to 30% of all homeowners, they must still pay taxes equaling about $300 per month.

Anyway you look at it, it takes money just to get through the month.

What are your monthly living expenses? How does it compare to the national averages? Are you overspending?

There are numerous cost of living calculators and information sources available on the Internet. Here are three good sites for information you need to become familiar with:

www.bankrate.com
www.homefair.com
www.bls.gov

I Hate Budgets

I don't want you to just get by, working the same old job, and perhaps having a little left over at the end of each month.

That's the kind of lifestyle they teach in budgeting books—and I hate budgeting books. Rather, I want you to get by, leave your job, and have enough cash left over to enjoy life and make bigger investments.

A great book to read on this subject is "The Richest Man in Babylon," by George Clason. It has been a bestseller for over 80 years and is readily available in most libraries and bookstores.

Now that you know I hate budgets, I want you to make one.

Not a budget that restricts your spending, but a budget that identifies where you stand today. What is the rock-bottom number of dollars it takes to get you through a month? This number should include your rent or mortgage, groceries, automobile expenses, and utilities.

By the way, I'm not talking about dinners in your favorite restaurant, movie rentals, and weekends at the lake.

Your Budget Overview

Housing Costs:

Utilities:

Groceries:

Insurance:

Auto & Gas:

Total:

This is the dollar amount I want you to focus on replacing through passive and portfolio income.

In the next chapter we will discuss how a lowly certificate of deposit can become your seeds of building wealth.

Millionaire Secret #2
Build a Nest Egg with Certificates of Deposit

Certificates of Deposit are lousy in terms of generating income, but they serve a crucial role in your wealth building efforts.

Once you have reined in your spending and found yourself with a little bit of spending cash at the end of the month, it's time to think in terms of protecting your growing cash reserves, and getting it to work for you.

After all, getting money to work for you, rather than you having to work for money, is what this book is all about.

Thus, the second step towards achieving wealth and finding financial freedom is to establish a nest egg of cold, hard cash equal to at least six months worth of your living expenses.

If you have done well with the first step, this should be easy—it just takes a little time. Again, to speed this process you may want to look into some home-based business ideas that can increase your income.

A Certificate Of Deposit Will Not Make You Wealthy, But...

Opening and holding a bank Certificate of Deposit (CD) is a great, and conservative, way to build a nest egg. Keep in mind however, with current interest rates, offset by taxes and a touch of inflation, your future value of money with CDs is not a way to get rich.

So, I am not asking you to expect CDs to make you wealthy. CDs are a perfect financial tool for securing money in a safe investment with a modest return. Money in your CD will always be there in case of an emergency, and the peace of mind it provides will motivate and encourage you to save and invest, and it will dramatically improve your self-confidence and outlook on life.

Two interesting places you may want to look to park your money, other than your bank or credit union, is Paypal.com and Etrade.com. Both offer some very competitive yields, without the time restrictions typically imposed on CDs (Warning: Keep in mind security risks of online investing).

Let me share a short story that I believe clarifies the role a CD can play in your wealth building efforts.

The Lack Of Money Destroys Lives

I recently overheard a cell phone conversation between a woman and her husband.

Apparently, he had recently lost his job and money was tight. I only heard her end of the conversation, but according to her a used car dealer they had dealt with needed forty dollars immediately, or he would repossess her car.

Imagine the stress, humiliation, and inconvenience the lack of forty dollars can place on your family. I never want to be in this position, and I don't want you to experience it either.

Spend less than you earn, and have the discipline to save what you don't spend. For you husbands, I hope you never have to tell your wife she has to give up her car. And for you wives, I hope your husband never faces the embarrassment of riding the bus or hitching a ride to work.

Don't punish yourselves like this.

A CD Represents Peace Of Mind

The easiest way to give yourself peace of mind, and a modicum of financial security, is to build a small nest egg of cash secured by a CD.

In my opinion, everybody should have about six months worth of living expenses locked away in a CD for emergency use.

For example, if it takes $2,500 per month to pay the bills and just get by, you should have at least $15,000 tucked away in a CD, prior to engaging in higher risk investments. Even when you begin to expand into stock market and real estate investments, maintain your $15,000 CD, and make all of your future investments pay for themselves, without dipping into your CD capital base.

Saving and holding onto six months worth of living expenses is hard, but to paraphrase W. Clement Stone, "If you can't save, the ability to create wealth is not within you."

Certificates of deposit are generally FDIC insured, which is certainly not the case for stock market and real estate investments. CDs also differ from money market accounts, so when you open a CD, make sure it falls under the FDIC umbrella. If you don't think FDIC insurance is important, consider what is happening in the lending markets right now.

Prior to opening your CD, you need to gather some facts about current yields and the time period you must keep your money locked in the CD. There are always ways to pull your funds out of a CD, but early withdrawal will carry penalties.

Know The Terms Of Your CD

You can get a great rundown on current CD rates and terms by reading Bankrate's CD Rate Trend Index. Check it out at www.bankrate.com. You may also want to see if your bank allows Add-Ons.

CDs with an Add-On feature allow you to open a CD with the minimal amount, and then add additional funds to the CD as they become available, while maintaining the original maturity date.

When investing in a CD, be aware of the length of time you are committing your money to. If the annual percentage yield (APY) for a six month CD is 4.9%, and a twelve month CD offers 5.1%, you will have decide if the extra return on investment (ROI) is worth having your money locked away an additional six months.

By using Bankrate's data, you can make this kind of decision based on their forecast for interest rate hikes or drops. If you expect interest rates to drop in the next six months you may want to go with the twelve month CD in order to lock in the better yield.

However, if rates are expected to go up, a six month term would allow you to reinvest at the higher rate. Additionally, if you are paying checking account fees at your bank, a CD puts you into a position to negotiate a reduction or elimination of the fees.

Talk to your banker, and be assertive. You deserve to be rewarded for your loyalty and your business.

The idea of purchasing CDs ties in with Secret #1, Spend Less Than You Earn.

Remember when I asked you to spend less than 90% of your current income? Well, CDs are a solid and safe way to move that 10-30% of your income out of harms way. This was my biggest challenge in achieving wealth.

If I had a dollar in my pocket, I always found a way to spend it. Finally, my wife took over the bank account, moved a percentage of my pay into a CD each month, and gave me a weekly allowance. It was humbling, but effective.

Today I thank her.

Use a CD to consistently squirrel away your extra income and you will have a sizable nest egg for both security and investment.

"Admittedly, with current interest rates, a certificate of deposit makes for a lousy investment.

However, the importance of opening and maintaining a CD cannot be over emphasized.

Building a nest egg equal to at least 6 months' of your living expenses will give you financial security, peace of mind, and foster the discipline you will need to build wealth."

The Millionaire's Secret

Millionaire Secret #3
Consumer Debt is Deadly

Consumer debt is a financial killer.

One of the best ways to reclaim your financial future is to repay those high interest consumer loans and then restrict the use of credit cards to emergencies and fast investment cash.

Therefore, the third step in creating wealth is to reduce your dependence on credit cards and ensure future monthly payments on all of your cards combined never exceeds 10% of your after tax income.

Dump The Doodad Shopping Mentality

If you shop for entertainment, you need to find a new hobby, today.

Consumer debt is usually used to finance the purchase of "nice to have" things--which typically depreciate in value. Whereas, investment debt is the use of financing to purchase things which go up in value, like real estate, antiques, and well-run businesses.

Consumer credit typically increases at an annual rate of about 2.5 percent, while revolving credit increases at an annual rate of 10 percent. However, due to the recent banking crisis, consumer credit decreased at an annual rate of 10.5 percent, revolving credit decreased at an annual rate of 8 percent, and non-revolving credit decreased at an annual rate of 11.75 percent, according to The Federal Reserve Statistical Release for July 2009.

Also indicative of our spending habits, Americans currently owe over 808 billion dollars in revolving debt, which is principally credit cards and auto loans, and over 1.3 trillion dollars in non-revolving debt.

According to U.S. Bankruptcy Court statistics, there were well over 2 million bankruptcy flings made annually, with the vast majority of these being non-business related filings. Remember, there are approximately 123 million working Americans; therefore, this number represents nearly 2 percent of the working population.

Investing Versus Spending

In my opinion, the abuse of credit cards by the American consumer has become a financial epidemic, and propensity of Americans to assume high interest credit card debt, while fearing the use of debt to make intelligent investments, is mind-boggling.

Consider this example. A new car may cost you up to $500 per month. At the end of 5 years, you will have a significantly depreciated car, with a loss of $30,000 or more in principal and interest payments.

Compare this to purchasing a rental property. In the worse case scenario, you may expect to make payments during vacancies, provide for unscheduled maintenance, and carry a negative cash flow from month to month. However, at the same time you will be enjoying a property that appreciates in value, while giving you a valuable tax write-off.

Appreciation and tax write-offs are not the primary reason to get involved in real estate, nor is carrying a negative cash flow a pleasant thought. But, in the long run, this is more advantageous to your wealth goals than the car loan.

As a credit consumer you should also protect yourself against the dreaded Universal Default Clause. Amazingly, a large percentage of major credit card issuers have this clause tucked into your user agreement.

Essentially, the Universal Default Clause allows your credit card company to significantly increase your interest rate and fees based on your credit score and payment history with other lenders, including your home and car loan. Watch out for this clause and try to avoid doing business with credit card companies that use this tactic to prey on their less sophisticated customers.

Is Real Estate A Safe Investment?

If you asked five people who are currently in foreclosure proceedings that question, you would get five resounding "not in my lifetime," type answers.

However, if you were to ask five investors who have recently scooped up bargain basement deals on rental properties that question, you would hear responses like, "give me more."

The point is, every investment is unique, and you should know your local market, understand the costs and risks involved, and always conduct due diligence prior to executing a deal.

Historically, real estate has been an excellent route towards creating wealth, and while current statistics relevant to foreclosures distort this perception of security, the number of investment properties entering foreclosure compared to the 2 million plus bankruptcy filings per year, suggests the risk to your financial well-being through real estate investment is lower than that of acquiring consumer debt.

Education in this area is critical to your success, so I strongly recommend you read books by real estate gurus like Robert Allen and Robert Kiyosaki before starting a property investment plan.

So, the next time you are tempted to take out a loan on a new boat or quad, consider how the cost of this purchase, with compounding interest, may be better used to achieve your financial goals.

The National Foundation for Credit Counseling believes it takes from 3 to 5 years to recover from credit card debt, once an individual starts a structured recovery plan. In short, consumer debt can put a severe damper on your wealth accumulation goals, and as you'll discover, accumulating wealth comes down to your willingness to delay gratification—a difficult emotion to master.

Over the years I have used credit cards for both consumer purchases and investments. Sadly, like many others, I also went through a stage in my life where I abused credit cards and allowed the balances due to become a burden to my family and a drain on my monthly income.

I used the first and second millionaire secrets in this book to dig myself out of debt, and have since limited myself to carrying a prepaid card. Normally, people use prepaid cards when they can't qualify for a regular credit card. However, the prepaid is also a great way to minimize your spending, as it only works when there is money in the bank to back up your purchases.

Drip By Drip, Credit Card Debt Adds Up

Credit card horror stories are everywhere, and there is a good chance you know somebody who has experienced something similar to the story below.

A young college student received a credit card offer in the mail. As a full-time student, he did not have a steady income and wondered how he managed to qualify. His credit rating was based entirely upon his potential to earn income as a future college graduate, and the complete lack of negative information in his file.

The student carried his freshly minted card in his pocket for several weeks, and resolved to never use it, except for an emergency.

Near the end of the semester he and a few classmates were pulling an all-night group study session in preparation for final exams. Around midnight somebody suggested they call out for pizza. They pooled around twelve dollars in cash between them and nearly gave up in frustration when our hapless credit worthy student volunteered his credit card.

It was a small beginning, as these things typically are, but credit use is like an addictive drug. It is so easy to use, and the pain of repayment is always somewhere down the road — too far away to be associated with the enjoyment of pizza tonight.

By the end of the school year, the student had accumulated over $1,000 in debt on his card. While his monthly payments remained small, they represented a significant strain on his budget. His monthly allowance from home was now being spent to make credit card payments, which meant he had to use the card to make more routine purchases.

The balance grew out of control, leading to a destroyed credit rating.

An Alternative Use Of Credit Card Debt

Another example of credit card use involved a young lady who worked a low paying job. She had dreams of a better life and spent a lot of her time looking for real estate investment opportunities. She carried four credit cards, with an available cumulative balance of around $12,000.

One day after work she came across a small house for sale by owner. It needed some work, but following an analysis of the market, she knew this home was worth more than the asking price. Using the cash option on her cards, she obtained $10,000 to make the down payment and cover closing costs. The owner carried the financing at a fair interest rate.

After closing she immediately set to work cleaning up the property. She then had it professionally appraised (insist on appraisals from Member Appraisal Institute) and listed for sale.

For three months she managed to make the minimum payments due on her cards before the house eventually sold for a modest profit. At closing the buyer assumed the loan due to the original owner, leaving a little less than $20,000 profit. She immediately paid off her balance due on all of her credit cards, and parked around $8,000 in her bank account.

While her return is not impressive to some investors, she did manage to make $8,000 out of nothing but information and gumption.

Both of these stories illustrate the power and dangers of credit card use. While it is not advisable to get involved in investments using credit cards, it is an option when quick cash is needed to capitalize on an opportunity.

Again, using credit cards to secure your investments is not advisable. The illustration above is only meant to show you how debt can either destroy or build your financial future.

Your Free Credit Report

As a wealth builder, it is vitally important that you monitor your credit report and correct any errors immediately. One of the easiest, and cheapest ways to obtain your personal credit report is over the Internet. It is estimated that up to 60% of all borrowers request a credit report at least once a year.

If you are trying to protect your privacy, you may want to be wary of the questions about your current address, phone number, employer, and other personal data they may ask in the "Request Your Credit Report Here" form.

A recent amendment to the federal Fair Credit Reporting Act requires each of the nationwide consumer reporting companies, Equifax, Experian, and TransUnion, to provide you with a free copy of your credit report, at your request, once every 12 months. Use the FTC government website www.annualcreditreport.com as your primary source for credit report data.

Now that you have learned about living on less than you earn, securing an emergency cash fund, and cutting consumer debt, it's time to burst your bubble on that job you hold.

"Consumer debt is a financial killer.

Until you learn to spend less than you earn, and avoid using consumer debt, such as high interest credit cards, you will not be able to achieve financial freedom.

Quite simply, to get ahead financially, you need to stop the shopping for fun habit in its tracks."

The Millionaire's Secret

Millionaire Secret #4
Your Job is a Wealth Inhibitor

Simply put, most jobs are not a route to wealth creation.

Your job is a necessary evil during the early stages of your wealth creation, but should not represent a long-term plan. Not only do jobs restrict your income potential, they may also be hazardous to future income.

Recent surveys and census data indicate approximately 30% of people will be forced to retire early due to circumstances beyond their control, including layoffs and illnesses. AXA Equitable and Nationwide Financial have an extensive database of figures related to forced layoffs and early retirements.

Jobs are created by entrepreneurs who understand that wealth is created by adding value to raw material or services, and selling finished products or services at a profit.

Who adds the value to raw materials and services?
You do.

And, you are only valuable to an employer when you can effectively and efficiently add value to the organization's product or service.

Thus, the fourth step in building personal wealth is to change your mindset about your employment status.

Don't Quit Your Day Job Just Yet

There's no denying the fact that a job, with a steady income, is nice to have. It helps you pay the bills and keeps a roof over your family's head. Unfortunately, that's about all it does.

What's in a job? Security? A pension? Some of us are dreaming of retirement, thinking we'll be happy living off half of what we can't afford to live on today.

A job was never meant to make people wealthy. In a free market environment we sell our labor to an employer for the highest pay possible, while your boss tries to pay you the lowest wage you will accept. Usually the boss wins, because he is in control of the purse strings.

As long as you look to your job for wealth, you will be disappointed.

Does A Job Equal Security?

Most Americans think a job is security, but they are wrong.

As long as you depend upon somebody else for your livelihood, you are a slave to that person and/or organization. And like a slave, you can be dispensed with as soon as they deem your services uneconomical.

It's a negative image, and I apologize for hitting you with it, but you can't sit back and relax in the pseudo security of a job or retirement plan and expect others to secure a financial future for you and your family.

Dependence is not security; independence is security.

While dropping my son off at school recently, I noticed an elderly gentleman standing in front of the school with a sandwich sign draped around his neck. The man was protesting unfair hiring practices by the school in the form of age discrimination.

We live in a society that rewards youth and beauty, while disregarding the value of experience and ability. This man was willing to stand before the community to protest this injustice.

His dilemma is all too common today, where hard working people have entrusted employers to provide them lifetime employment. Unfortunately, this trust does not reflect reality.

Stepping Outside The "Job" Box

Owning your own business is one vehicle you can use to take responsibility for your own financial future, without having to depend upon the vagaries of an unjust job market.

The expression, "if you want to catch fish, you have to risk the bait," is so common it has become cliché. But how many of us actually incorporate that basic philosophy into our lives?

Are you willing to risk the "security" of the traditional nine to five, Monday through Friday routine, to enjoy financial freedom?

Vince Lombardi once stated "the will to excel, the will to win: these are the things that endure." A business built with your own hands, energy, and ingenuity can endure where a job cannot, but if you expect to become a successful entrepreneur, you will have to take risks.

These risks do not mean senseless gambling of your savings in the stock or bond markets, or betting everything on a horse race. Taking a risk means putting your self-confidence and self-image on the line. It means taking the chance of being embarrassed in the marketplace. And, it can also mean going against popular opinion and peer pressure to follow a dream.

As Teddy Roosevelt was fond of saying, "seek opportunity, not security."

Aside from the "job security" issues, your status as a wage or salary earner places you in the highest taxed form of income. Passive and portfolio income does not fall victim to Social Security taxes, and expenses associated with operating your business come out of your gross receipts prior to taxes.

The structure of business taxation can allow you to enjoy some of the finer things in life, such as dining out, vacations, and nice cars (provided they are legitimate business expenses), while the same pleasures in life for a wage earner must use after tax dollars to do so.

Robert Kiyosaki talks about this concept in detail in his Rich Dad, Poor Dad series, which should be required reading for any wealth builder. You don't have to like him, agree with him, or buy real estate to get wealthy, but you should at least give him a try.

Not convinced? Take a look at some current statistics regarding employment.

A Few Job Statistics To Think About

It's been said that 80% of America is two missed paychecks away from financial disaster, and recent statistics indicate Americans spend 110% of their monthly income.

Do you fit this mold?

What would happen if you were laid off without pay tomorrow? Can Americans look forward to a secure retirement under Social Security or the company pension plan?

Current labor statistics do not paint a pretty picture, with quality jobs being outsourced overseas quicker than new jobs are being created. Sure, there are always low paying, low skill jobs available. But who can support a family on minimum wage?

Manufacturing jobs in particular have taken a beating in the marketplace during the past few decades, with some states, like Michigan, losing over 23,000 jobs in the course of a year. According to Labor Department figures, 26 states have seen manufacturing job losses in the past year.

The federal government claims many of these displaced workers are receiving retraining, however, Bureau of Labor Statistics suggest only a fraction of those laid off receive commercially valuable retraining. And of those that do, many or the job training programs are for short-term, government or community based jobs, such as Census workers and community organizers.

The Bureau of Labor Statistics defines displaced workers as, "persons 20 years of age and older who lost or left jobs because their plant or company closed or moved, there was insufficient work for them to do, or their position or shift was abolished." During the first few years of this decade, 5.3 million workers were displaced from jobs they had held for at least 3 years.

Your Future As An Employee

In June of 2006, 4.6% of the available workforce in America was unemployed for an average of 18.4 weeks. For workers over 45 years of age, this unemployment period jumped to 23.8 weeks. That is over 5 months without pay.

Compare this to the statistic in the Introduction of this book that reveals many Americans have less than 3 months worth of cash and assets available to sustain them without continuing income. Of course, there is unemployment insurance, but this may take weeks to kick in, is a degrading and frustrating process, and is certainly no route to achieving the standard of living your family deserves.

Of the 7.6 million Americans unemployed at one time or another in the past year, 4.3 million lost their job due to completion of temporary projects, 3.7 million were laid off, and 1.9 suffered permanent job loss through no apparent fault of their own.

To top it off, the median weekly wage and salary for working Americans is around $651. It hardly seems worth the effort.

Yet, 123 million American go to work everyday, living paycheck to paycheck. Over 13 million of these people work in "alternative" job arrangements as independent contractors, on-call laborers, and temporary services. Additionally, nearly 8 million Americans work multiple jobs simultaneously — just to make ends meet.

It's Time To Get Excited

Success gurus like Anthony Robbins and Robert Kiyosaki teach that you have to get excited about wealth building to achieve success.

What excites you about building personal wealth? How do you feel about poverty, or the lack of money? What motivates you to spend your free time reading books like this, studying interest rate tables, or analyzing stocks and real estate deals?

To achieve financial success you must get emotionally charged over something wealth represents. After all, it's probably not the money you are after. You are after the security and promise of a better life.

Use these emotional tags to drive you to work while others sleep. Use your anger over working for an unappreciative boss to push you to limit your spending on frivolous doodads. Use your desire to achieve a better quality of life for your family as an impetus to analyze more deals, take calculated risks, and strive for more sources of passive and portfolio income.

If all else fails, use your determination to achieve the independence and security of sound financial management and personal wealth as your motivation to get out and make something happen for yourself.

"Your job was never intended to help you create wealth.

In fact, the last thing an employer wants is for you to gain independence and no longer add value to his or her service or product.

Go ahead and work to get by, but devote your free time to working for yourself and your future."

The Millionaire's Secret

There is a Degree of Risk in Creating Wealth

Wealth builders are risk takers. But not in the sense of risk taking you may think.

The key to creating wealth, while minimizing your exposure to risk is to embrace what I call "measured risk" through knowledge of your market niche and understanding the associated opportunity costs of not making selected business decisions or investments.

"Opportunity Costs" is a fancy word used to measure the "loss" of income or revenue by "not" making a specific investment or business decision. Bean counters like to use opportunity costs to measure upside and downside potential of business transactions, and recognize that any business deal can incur risk of loss.

Again, risk does not mean gambling.

Learning How To Embrace And Control Risk

Risk is the probability of a loss, and its potential impact on your financial well-being. Successful entrepreneurs mitigate that risk by learning everything they can about an investment or business venture — this is called due diligence — before they get involved.

Perfect knowledge is not always available, as every endeavor has unknowns; however, your job is to analyze the information that is available, and then make informed decisions.

Some risk can be reduced by "hedging;" whereby, the risk taker invests in insurance policies, or more conservative investments, to minimize the risk exposure.

Hedging costs money in the form of insurance premiums, and lower return on investments. For example, an investment in a bank certificate of deposit is considered very safe, but its returns are currently averaging less than 3-5% per year. At the same time, an investment in a less conservative — and thus more risky — real estate transaction, may net a gain of 100% or more.

Every investor must determine his or her own tolerance for risk exposure and make investment decisions accordingly.

Another form of risk is evident in "gambling," where the gambler is willing to lose his or her entire investment in pursuit of a huge payoff.

The lottery is a perfect example of this.

If you buy a one-dollar lottery ticket, your entire investment of that dollar will be reduced to zero value if the numbers you selected are not picked by the lottery system. Lotteries typically have astronomical odds against the gambler, with 100 million to 1 odds being common. Your risk exposure in this area is extremely high, but may be mitigated by limiting the amount you routinely spend on lottery tickets.

Are You A Risk Seeker?

A business transaction or investment that offers the chance to win big, countered by the more likely chance of losing your entire investment, is essentially gambling.

Some people actually thrive on taking risk, and are considered "risk seekers." This is obviously not for the faint of heart, nor is it advisable to risk next month's rent in pursuit of a get-rich-quick scheme.

"Risk averse" people are the exact opposite, and run from any sort of identifiable risk in a business or investment venture. The happy hunting grounds lie somewhere between being risk seeking and risk averse. Finding this center ground is dependent upon your unique circumstances, available financial resources, and your ability to manage risk.

Once you have addressed the question of risk, you will need to consider how fear of failure may be impacting your progress towards your financial goals.

"Taking risks does not mean gambling your future on the roll of a dice.

Rather, as investors and entrepreneurs, your job is to understand and control the risks by conducting due diligence in all of your transactions and plans.

Know what you are getting into. The old adage "look before you leap" is very relevant here."

The Millionaire's Secret

Millionaire Secret #6
Wealth and the Fear of Failure

What is fear of failure, and why does it hold so many of us back?

Fear of failure comes in many forms, but it can basically be distilled down to two key areas:

1. Fear of financial loss
2. Fear of embarrassment

The best way to overcome fear is to combine knowledge with planning and action.

Whatever investment or business opportunity decision you are facing, get the facts, plan your course of action, and take action--that is: plan your work, and work your plan. Nothing beats fear like bold action.

The alternative to action is to stay where you are. If you are happy with your current socio-economic status, then you have nothing to fear, because you will never take the risks or encounter the danger of failure.

Failing Your Way To Financial Success

Popular success literature frequently touts the advantages of failure, and to a certain degree I agree with their philosophy of "failing your way to success." However, the one element that is often overlooked in deriving a benefit from failure is the need to learn from failure.

If you engage in a given business transaction and fail, you must learn and remember the hard lessons of this failure to prevent making the same mistakes over and over.

Therefore, the sixth step in your quest for financial freedom is to learn how to fail—constructively.

When Thomas Edison conducted over 10,000 experiments to perfect the light bulb, he did not look at the failed experiments as "failures," rather, each experiment demonstrated how not to make a light bulb.

Failure for Edison was a learning experience, which he capitalized on to bring light to the world. In a sense, his experiments were the epitome of the maxim "try, try, again," exemplified in this quote by Buckminster Fuller: "Whatever humans have learned had to be learned as a consequence only of trial and error experience. Humans have learned only through mistakes."

Edison's experiences are also indicative of a critical difference in attitudes among successful versus unsuccessful people.

The Fear Of Failure And Learning From Your Mistakes

Like Edison, successful people view mistakes as results, such as the testing of hypotheses in an experiment, while unsuccessful people see mistakes as a permanent result, unworthy of further effort.

The fear of failure may also be rooted in a natural human fear of the unknown. Any business venture or investment holds an element of risk, and as the limits to that risk become uncertain, or poorly defined, you may find yourself becoming more fearful of getting involved.

This is a normal, and prudent, emotion. As an entrepreneur you need to work harder to quantify that risk. Always ask yourself, what is the worse case scenario for this business opportunity? If the worse case scenario is tolerable, based on your financial and emotional strength, than there is no reason not to attempt it.

If however, the worse case scenario is intolerable, you must do something to reduce the risk or level of potential loss before getting involved.

The Role Of Goal Setting In Creating Wealth

Another impediment to progress is the setting of unrealistic goals. Goals can become overwhelming to the point that they make you fearful of getting started.

For example, if you have written a goal to invest in 10 income-producing houses within the next year, the daunting task of finding and purchasing 10 houses may subconsciously sabotage your efforts to get started.

Perhaps a better way to approach such a goal is to set a goal to buy 1 income producing property within the next 60 days. After achieving that goal, immediately set another goal to buy another property.

Other than property investments, many wealth builders pursue their dreams by starting their own businesses. As in goal setting, starting a business itself can be a daunting task, and may create an element of fear due to the rate of business failures you frequently hear about.

Internal Revenue Service statistics indicate there were 18.6 million firms with no employees, and 7.2 million firms with employees. Combined, these firms contributed 23 billion dollars paid in taxes to the federal government.

Are You Willing To Fail?

According to the Bureau of the Census, two-thirds of new employer establishments survive at least two years, and 44 percent survive at least four years. Over the past decade, small business net job creation fluctuated between 60 and 80 percent. While the exact numbers are hard to pin down, approximately 81% of new businesses close shop within the first year, and of those, around 6% declare bankruptcy.

The numbers may appear frightful, but in the grand scheme of things the risks of owning a small business are no worse than most human endeavors.

As you can see, the business of America is business, with small business owners leading the way. Despite the projections of failure, our economy and government thrive on small business start-ups.

In the end, it is not the number of times you fail that counts, but the number of times you succeed.

Consider Hank Aaron. He struck out far more times than he hit homeruns. Was he a failure? Is he remembered for striking out?

In another example, the pro cycling Tour de France is a 21-stage event. It is quite common in this stage race for the overall winner of the race to not win any of the individual stages. Does that make the race winner a loser?

As in most walks of life, the end result is more important than the so-called failures on the way to success, and upon closer inspection, you will note that successful people are action oriented.

"I've learned to fear regret more than failure.

If you allow the fear of failure to stop you from taking action to improve yourself, there will come a time when you will regret having not tried."

The Millionaire's Secret

Millionaire Secret #7
Wealth Building Requires Personal Action

Modern American society has become one of dependence.

We have become spoiled by government handouts and ideologies that say, "Society owes us."

Society owes you nothing, and sadly, nobody but your spouse and mother give a damn if you are successful or not. In fact, your spouse and mother may like the idea of you working in a "steady" and "secure" job your entire life.

If you wish to become a successful business owner, you must decide right now that you are the only one that can make it possible. Don't wait for the lottery, and don't dwell on your misfortunes. This is self-pity, and it will get you nowhere.

As we stated earlier, most successful people have buckets of failures in their lives. The difference is, they keep trying, while failures give up or never try in the first place.

To become successful, stop whining about the status quo, your upbringing, and the odds stacked against you. Pick up your shovel and start digging yourself out of the rut, today.

So, the seventh step to achieving wealth beyond reason is to accept personal responsibility for your own success.

Taking Responsibility For Your Life

What does it mean to "accept personal responsibility" for your life?

In the context of this book, accepting personal responsibility means:

- Recognizing that you are in charge of your life, which includes the choices and goals you set for yourself.
- Acknowledging the decisions you make as yours, and any credit for success, or blame for failure, rests entirely upon you.
- Taking care of your physical and mental health.
- Understanding that nobody cares about your financial future as much as you do.

Therefore, the impetus to achieve your financial goals must come from you. Nobody else is responsible for motivating you to succeed.

Accepting personal responsibility has many rewards, including a sense of self-reliance, rugged individualism, and the satisfaction of cutting your own trail through life.

On the other hand, refusing to accept personal responsibility can hurt you in a number of ways.

Failure to accept personal responsibility can:

- Foster of an attitude of dependency upon others.
- Destroy your ability to create and maintain positive relationships with others.
- Set you up for failure when your network of supporters tires of propping you up.
- Sabotage your ability to deal with fear and the uncertainty of the marketplace.
- Cause your physical and mental health to deteriorate.

People who are overly dependent upon others typically feel life is unfair, have a negative outlook on life and the opportunities life offers, and frequently place blame for their personal on others.

None of these characteristics are conducive to the wealth building process.

Finding The Motivation To Succeed

As a wealth builder, I had to learn to look inward for motivation and ideas. While it is helpful to maintain relationships with professionals, and to depend upon them for advice on such things as taxes, legal issues, and health matters, this does not excuse you from exhausting all of your personal resources prior to seeking help.

For example, I use an accountant to assist with my taxes, but throughout the year I maintain accurate records of my profit and losses, and strive to keep abreast of changing laws that may impact my tax status. And when it comes to health, I try to exercise regularly and eat a balanced diet. Yet every couple years I get a physical.

Goal Setting Revisited

So, how do you become more responsible for your life?

You start by setting realistic goals and mapping out specific plans of action to achieve these goals. Follow this with the recognition that you alone are responsible for achieving these goals, and make the deliberate decision to work towards your goals.

I have found that with clearly defined goals, the motivation and energy to assume personal responsibility falls into place with mathematical precision.

Millionaire Secret #8

Creating Personal Wealth is a Numbers Game

If you can create enough sources of cash flow, outside your normal day job, you can realistically replace the need for a full time job.

Imagine, making the same money you make working 40 plus hours a week, dealing with traffic jams daily, putting up with slobs, and stressing over job security, without the headaches and hassles.

Is it possible?

Yes.

Therefore, the eighth step in your progression to personal wealth is to crunch the numbers, start small, and dream big.

Building Wealth On Small Successes

One of my favorite pastimes is to crunch business opportunity and income producing numbers. If I wanted to replace a job that provided me with a $40,000 gross (before taxes) annual income, I would need to make $3,333 dollars per month, $769 per week, or $109 per day.

Hey, this is fun.

I only need enough alternative forms of income to generate $109 per day, and I could spend my future enjoying life, expanding my business ventures, and investing wisely for a secure future for my family.

For this example, let's think in terms of a round number, say $100.

What could you do to create $100 of cash flow into your hip national bank 365 days per year?

One hundred dollars may sound like a lot to make each and every day, using your own wits and not depending on a government handout or an employer's paycheck, but it is a realistic number, starting from where you are at today.

I will not ask you to spend 40 plus hours a week hustling around town bothering people, or engaging in illegal or unethical activities. You can do this honestly and be proud to share your moneymaking ideas with your mother.

Consider this example. If you sold a product online for $10, you would only need to sell 10 units to make $100. If your item sold for $25, you would only need to sell 4 units. Or, if you sold a product for $769 profit, you would only have to sell one unit per week.

Using the vast array of mediums to market and sell products today, you could feasibly replace your job income with a fraction of the time and effort you expend serving the goals and dreams of your employer.

As in any business venture, there are risks, setbacks, and disappointments. However, if you will use due diligence in all of your decisions, seek expert advice whenever possible, and persist while others dropout or quit, you can do this.

You need to start by reading more about this concept. I recommend you read these books immediately:

The Automatic Millionaire, by David Bach
Rich Dad, Poor Dad, by Robert Kiyosaki
Multiple Streams of Income, by Robert G. Allen

A Plan, An Idea, And Bold Action Is All It Takes

It has been said that we are what we eat. This may be true, but I believe we are also what we dream. What are your dreams? Your goals? Your ambitions?

Finding success in any business endeavor begins with a dream, which must then be developed into concrete goals, as I discuss in the Life Plan Worksheet later in this book.

Once you have established specific goals, break these goals into tasks, and then into steps. For example, if you have a dream to create an income outside your primary job, this dream could become a goal to make $20,000 profit per year selling products on Ebay.

This goal could then be broken into tasks of identifying a hot product line, finding sources for your merchandise, and learning how to become a Powerseller on Ebay.

I use Ebay as an example only. There are dozens of other online opportunities available.

At this point in the goal setting process you must transform the tasks into steps. One step may be to visit local auctions and thrift shops for merchandise, another step may be to open Ebay and Paypal accounts, followed by actually listing items for sale, shipping the products and providing customer service.

Each step in this process must be deliberately accomplished to achieve success, but it all starts with a dream. Therefore, we are what we dream.

As a home-based entrepreneur you need to take a look at a variety of opportunities. Keep your expenditures and fees low, if not zero, and then choose 1-3 ideas that you feel would inspire you to take action.

Fortunes have been made on one idea, cleverly marketed, produced, and delivered to the customer.

Millionaire Secret #9

Use Other Peoples' Time and Money

While the previous principle states that you must take action for yourself, please do not interpret this to mean "by yourself."

Capitalism and personal wealth are built on the concepts of labor utilization and capital investment. In other words, using people and their money to build your empire.

Note that I did not say "abusing" people and their money. When you use people you treat them fairly and with respect. When you use other people's money, you repay it, with interest.

The service industry provides a clear example of this concept.

Creating Wealth Using "People" Leverage

If the owner of a security agency is able to charge $20 per hour for security services, and pay his or her labor $10 per hour, plus an estimated 25% of gross labor costs in social security and worker's compensation payments, the owner of this agency is able to realize $7.50 per hour in gross profit.

If the agency was able to land contracts sufficient to bill for say, 10,000 hours in a month, he or she could see over $75,000 per month in gross profit. This is the power of leverage in the form of utilizing the talents and resources of other people.

This concept befuddles the professional sector, such as doctors, dentists, and lawyers, who can only bill for services they personally provide.

Thus, the ninth step in acquiring wealth is to use other people's time and money in an ethical and fair manner.

Creating Wealth Using "Financial" Leverage

Consider a similar case of using borrowed money to make investments. If you had $10,000 to invest in a piece of income producing real estate, how much property could you control? There are some zero down deals out there, but generally, the down payment is going to represent about 10% of the property value.

Therefore, your $10,000 nest egg will control a $100,000 property. Rent on this property will average in the neighborhood of 1% of the value, so you may see $1,000 per month in rental income.

In this scenario, you have successfully used $90,000 of other people's money to buy and control this property. What if you were able to obtain a loan for 100% of the property value?

With zero upfront cash invested, and a positive cash flow from rents, (with a breakeven scenario at minimum, keeping in mind maintenance costs and potential vacancies) your return on investment (ROI) is infinite.

With any real estate transaction, due diligence and professional assistance is critical to your success.

Seeking professional assistance is a perfect example of leveraging yourself by utilizing the talents and skills of other people.

A typical lawyer has spent approximately 6-7 years in college, three of those dedicated to the study of law. When you seek a lawyer's advice, you are paying for access to this knowledge — a small fee compared to the alternative of years of your life spent in training, or hefty lawsuits from disregarding the law.

Likewise, the careful use of associates can propel your personal financial rocket into the stratosphere. Consider the example of the referral marketing business model, known as network marketing.

Through network marketing you are able to multiply your efforts to sell products through a team of like-minded associates. One look at the top income earners reported by www.businessforhome.org will show you how powerful this concept can be.

This is the power of the leverage and the wealth building potential inherent to using other peoples' time and talents. And by the way, using the leverage of other people's time and money creates financial empires.

When an empire builder uses other people's money and labor he multiplies his potential, much like a hand tool magnifies the strength and utility of your hand.

Could you imagine taking lug nuts off your car without a wrench? Likewise, can you imagine building a business without the services of other people, the advice of legal and accounting professionals, or the backing of venture capitalists or lenders?

"The exploitation of people, or the taking of money with no intent to repay is wrong.

However, the fair use of other people's time and money is ethical, and is the key to building wealth in a capitalistic society."

The Millionaire's Secret

Millionaire Secret #10
Stay Positive and Enthusiastic

Negative dead heads are everywhere.

Unfortunately, many of them are the people that love you the most.

People don't consciously destroy other people's dreams, but if you're not careful, all the good Samaritans around you will convince you that you cannot get ahead.

But don't be too quick to blame others. In actuality, we are our worst enemies. Lack of confidence, a bad attitude, and self-criticism is more harmful than exposure to negative people, and must be overcome if you expect to find the motivation to master a market niche or climb the obstacles to success.

Wealth And Your Mental Mindset

Recent bestselling books, such as "The Secret," and "The Law of Attraction," reflect the continued popularity of this subject. While positive thinking in itself will not make you wealthy, a good attitude, peppered with a dose of self-confidence, is the tenth step in your success ladder.

In Richard Bach's story *Jonathan Livingston Seagull*, Jonathan is ostracized for attempting to do things that normal seagulls shouldn't do.

His attempt to get ahead and prosper is scorned by the other seagulls until he is banned from the flock. Flying alone, he discovers the joys of life outside the realm of rotten fish and crowded beaches.

While this book is about 35 years old, its message is relevant to your pursuit of wealth today. I strongly recommend you buy a used copy from Amazon (by the way, selling used books on Amazon is a great home-based business).

Richard Bach's story is a metaphor for man and holds valuable lessons for all of us.

Are you struggling to rise above the crowd? Or to separate yourself from mediocrity and failure?

The harder you try, the more people will tell you it's impossible. Misery loves company, and the last thing people want is to see you rise above them.

Your job is to ignore the negative dead heads and remain focused on your goals.

Where do you get your information? Whose advice do you seek and/or follow? Where and how do you spend your free time? Who do you associate with?

The answers to these questions can be revealing and disturbing.

You may want to adopt these personal rules:

- Accept business and investment advice only from people who are currently making at least twice what you make.
- Do not let failures tell you how to succeed.
- Do not accept the opinions of losers as gospel.
- Do not spend your time with losers or unmotivated people.
- Do the most productive thing possible at any given time.

Yes, A Positive Mental Attitude Is Important

The best way I know to keep a positive mental attitude, and stay on track with your wealth building program, is to model yourself after successful people. Join clubs like Rotary International, Toastmasters International, The Jaycees, your local Chamber of Commerce, or whatever professional organization is in your community.

I'm not suggesting you join them all, just join one or two and become a reliable, active member. You'll rub shoulders with the doers in your community, meet influential people, and see success in action.

An element of positive thinking is the reliance upon luck for your success. While luck has its place in any endeavor, people are often misguided by their definition of luck.

Luck is a nickname for hard work, perseverance, and making the right choices relevant to opportunities. Plain and simple, counting on luck is for losers. I believe luck comes to those who prepare for it.

How do you prepare for luck?

You prepare for luck by educating yourself about the business and investment opportunities you're interested in, focusing your energies and financial resources on building your empire, and being at the port when your ship comes in.

The bottom line: Don't count on luck to make you wealthy. Successful people make their own luck. They don't wait for it.

"Having a positive mental attitude will not create success or financial wealth in itself.

However, a good attitude will see you through the tough times and motivate you to keep trying while others have long since packed their bags and gone home."

The Millionaire's Secret

Millionaire Secret #11
Create Passive and Portfolio Income

The true meaning of wealth is freedom.

- Freedom to choose when and where you will spend your life.
- Freedom to choose whom you will spend your life with.
- Freedom to buy the things that make life pleasant, and to travel to the places others only dream about.

In short, wealth gives you time freedom.

Wealth is not the money in your bank account, but the freedom that money gives you.

Creating Wealth Using Automatic Pilots

If you ever wish to free yourself from the chains of slave labor you must first establish automatic pilots. Automatic pilots are investments and businesses that essentially run themselves or are run by others while still managing to throw off income to you.

Owning a piece of rental property managed by an agent and creating a positive cash flow is an example of an autopilot.

Thus, step eleven in the wealth building process is to create passive and portfolio income.

I know a young man in my community who purchased four single-family homes, became licensed by the county to operate the homes as group homes for developmentally disabled adults, and recruited and trained staff to run the homes.

Less than five years later he is a multi-millionaire, and rarely spends more than 10 hours per month monitoring his business.

Not every business is suited for absentee ownership, and tight control mechanisms must be put into place; but, the potential for wealth creation in businesses that do not require the owner's presence is phenomenal.

If you could do something to create an automatic pilot that gave you $100 per month, could you repeat it? How many $100 a month autopilots will it take to equal your current income?

Automatic pilots are the true representation of wealth because they provide you with an income, while allowing you the freedom to enjoy it.

As stated earlier, passive and portfolio income is generally created from the ownership or control of assets, including those listed below:

- Income producing real estate

- Stocks and bonds
- Interest from savings
- Royalties from intellectual property

Your challenge in this important step is to figure out how and where to acquire income producing assets.

It doesn't happen by spending more than you earn, failing to save and build a capital base, or spending your saved money foolishly on worthless doodads that depreciate the moment you purchase them.

Creating automatic pilots is the essence of Warren Buffett's philosophy of investment. While he remains highly involved in the day-to-day activities of his businesses and investments, Buffett has created multiple streams of income, becoming a billionaire in the process.

In a previous principle I discussed how a hypothetical security guard firm could create wealth for the owner. Taken a step further, the business owner could recruit and train a manager to oversee the daily activity of this business. He could also contract with an accountant to do his billing, taxes, and payroll.

Control Mechanisms Are Crucial

The long-term success of operating a hands-off business like this will be contingent on the owner's creation of an operations manual, enforcement of quality standards, and strict billing and payroll control mechanisms. This is doable, and happens every day in the business world.

Robert Kiyosaki repeatedly makes this point in his Rich Dad, Poor Dad books.

According to Kiyosaki, you don't want to create a job for yourself by opening a business, and then structuring it where you will have to be there to ensure the work gets done.

Your objective should be to create a business, and then set controls in place so you can enjoy the profits of that business with minimal personal input.

Using due diligence, start today to find and obtain a piece of real estate that will throw off a positive cash flow each month. Do not accept a negative cash flow situation, as this will stymie your ability to make further investments.

Also, do some research on the stock market and find a solid company with growth potential and a history of paying dividends to park some of your money in.

Use the positive cash flow from your real estate and stocks to make further investments, and never touch your capital base.

Millionaire Secret #12
Set Realistic and Challenging Goals

The idea of setting goals is nothing new and you have probably heard it before. But do you do it?

Amazingly, less than 3% of the population sets financial goals.

In 1954 an interesting experiment was conducted at Yale University. The graduating class was surveyed and it was determined that only 3% of the class population had written financial goals. Twenty years later the resurveyed this same group of people. The results were astounding.

The 3% that had set financial goals in 1954 had a net worth greater than the combined net worth of the remaining 97% of the class population.

The lack of goals will not guarantee failure, but with numbers like those above, why risk it? And because I like putting the odds of success in my favor, rather than working against myself and good advice, setting realistic and challenging goals is the twelfth step to financial freedom.

If you want to learn how to set goals, read *See You at the Top*, by Zig Ziglar.

Assets Alone Do Not Create Wealth

Acquiring assets in themselves is not a viable goal towards achieving sustainable wealth.

According to the IRS, for people in America with gross assets in excess of $675,000, over 32,000 held a negative net worth, 3 million people had a net worth of less than 1 million dollars, and approximately 2.4 million held a net worth above 1 million dollars.

Clearly, owning or controlling assets does not equate to net worth.

Nearly 1.4 million people had succeeded in acquiring large amounts of assets, but had offsetting liabilities to nullify their wealth positions.

Assets create wealth when, and only when, they throw off positive cash flow, sufficient to meet all debt, taxes, insurance, maintenance, management, and service expenses related to the asset.

With this in mind, be sure your goals and action plans define how you will generate income, how you will invest and spend this income, and ultimately, how you will define success in your wealth building goals.

An important step in this process is to visualize what success and wealth means to you.

After you have established your goals in writing it helps to visualize what the achievement of these goals will bring you. For example, if you have set a goal of attaining sales commissions of $10,000 per month, imagine what

$10,000 a month will do for your investment plans and lifestyle. Picture yourself standing in line at the bank waiting to cash that big check, or paying cash for a new car.

A New Way To Think About Goal Setting

For most people writing down, or even following goals, is about as exciting as grocery shopping with a fixed budget and a list. Sure, it makes sense, but it turns the shopping experience into a chore rather than a mini adventure of discovery.

I believe this reticence to set or follow goals comes from an innate disgust with plans. There is something in the human psyche that objects to any hint of predestination or predetermination. That is, we intuitively despise being told what we can and cannot do, or what our limits may be.

I've experienced the same reluctance about goal setting that you may be feeling. But let me tell you how one short book changed the way I look at goal setting.

In Viktor Frankl's book, *Man's Search for Meaning*, Frankl discusses many of the misguided myths associated with goal setting. According to Frankl, it is not enough to merely focus on goals, and may in fact be counter-productive.

Instead, Frankl suggests you focus on the individual steps necessary to achieve your goal. For example, if you wanted to realize $1,000 per month in automatic pilot type income, it may be more productive to concentrate on first achieving $100 per month in income. Frankl further suggests the goal itself be forgotten, with your energy being better suited towards doing the daily chores and tasks to achieve the goal.

In practical terms, if you wanted to own a rental property, saving for the upfront expenses, researching your market, and learning about property management, would al be daily tasks that move you in the direction of successfully owning and operating a rental property.

Frankl's methodology could also be applied to a weight-loss program. Rather than focus on losing, say 25 pounds, you would be better served to focus on eating the right foods and getting the right amount of exercise—today.

Taking it one day at a time, you will lose weight, building on the small successes one day at a time.

For many people, wealth means freedom from a boring job, or the ability to jump on an airplane and fly to Europe, just because they want to. Whatever your dreams, write them down (goals), and then imagine yourself already enjoying them (visualization).

When it comes to achieving a goal, committing yourself to that goal is the first major step towards receiving it, and visualizing your goal is the second step.

Success Takes Bold Action

Goals and plans are only half the battle, however. General Patton lived by the belief that bold action, however flawed, beats the best of plans with little or no action.

Many of us are guilty of being all plan, and no action-- and we're doomed to failure because of it.

Even the best of plans are worthless without action. If you want to create wealth you must do something different than you've been doing. Consider what you have accomplished in the past five years. Does it meet with your approval? If not, it may be time to change your habits and your thinking.

It may be time to throw out long held opinions and practices and try something else. One thing is sure, if you continue doing the same things you have been doing, five years from now you will be in the same position you are today.

Excuses Are Everywhere

Some of the more common excuses for not getting started include one's age, race, or educational level. However, businesses are successfully owned and operated by Americans of all ages, race, and educational level.

According to the U.S. Census Bureau, 67% of all business owners reported their business provided their primary source of income. 24% of business owners claimed they did not have a high school level education at the startup of their business, while 26% claimed some college, and 43% stated they had a college degree. Proving it is never too late to start, 63% of all businesses are owned by people over the age of 45, with many of these being in the over 65 category.

Additionally, women are excelling in business today. According to statistics published by the Census Bureau in 2006, "Women owned 6.5 million nonfarm U.S. businesses, employing 7.1 million persons and generating $940.8 billion in business revenues."

Putting It All Together

The next page of this book may well be the most important one of all. We have all read and heard about putting our goals in writing, but this critical step in the wealth building process is often neglected.

After learning about Viktor Frankl's concept of Logotherapy, I relegated the goal setting process to hogwash and wishful thinking. However, Frankl changed my mind about goals by suggesting the goal setter focus less on the overall goal and more on the individual tasks and steps required to stay on track to achieve a goal.

Your Life Plan Worksheet

Borrowing from this concept, I developed a Life Plan Worksheet that helped me visualize how my daily activities helped or hindered my progression. Take a few minutes and think about your dreams and how these can be translated into measurable and achievable goals.

Remember, don't make the mistake of being "all plan and no action." Stay focused on the daily activities and steps you must take to achieve your goals.

The Life Plan Worksheet leads off with Dreams and Goals, but this is only to serve the purpose of helping you identify specific steps and actions required to achieve those goals and realize that big dream. Once you have identified the steps you should take, focus on them, not the overall goal.

As Frankl taught us, if the activities contribute towards moving you closer to the goal, then you will reach your goal, without thinking about it.

LIFE PLAN WORKSHEET

Many of us devote more time to planning vacations than we do planning our lives. Use this Life Plan Worksheet to develop specific steps you can take to achieve a goal that will help you and your family achieve the life of your dreams. Life planning all begins with a dream.

DREAM

Write one sentence that best states an ideal lifestyle for you.

I have a dream to…

GOAL

Write a one-sentence goal statement that will help you realize your dream. A written goal should be specific, and include numbers and a realistic date of accomplishment.

To live the life of my dreams I will…

TASKS

Break your goal statement into 3-5 tasks you must accomplish to achieve your goal.

To meet my goal I will complete the following tasks within a specified time:

1.

2.

3.

STEPS

Write 3-5 steps you must take to complete each of the above tasks.

List the steps necessary to successfully complete each of the tasks listed above.

Steps 1-3 of first task:

Steps 1-3 of second task:

Steps 1-3 of third task:

Millionaire Secret #13
Remember Income Limiters

No wealth-building plan is complete without considering taxes and inflation.

Your investment decisions should always be tempered with the question: How will this investment be affected by taxes and inflation?

The tax man cometh. Therefore, the thirteenth step to financial freedom is to become wise to the tax man's ways and adjust your investment and business decisions accordingly. Ideally of course, you want to minimize your dependence on employment income (as this is taxed the highest), and build passive and portfolio income.

For example, if you put $10,000 in a savings account at 5% interest, at the end of one year you would have accrued $500 in interest. If at the same time the economy was enjoying a low inflation rate of 3%, your purchasing power with a nest egg of $10,500 would be around $10,150, a loss of $350. Also, state and federal income taxes may take an additional $50 to $150 of your profits away from you.

Taxes And Inflation Are Wealth Destroyers

Here are some more inflation facts. $5,000 in 1980 has the same buying power in 2006 as $12,311. That's more than twice your initial amount. To put it in practical terms, $5,000 would buy about 10,000 gallons of gasoline in 1980, and less than 1,600 gallons in 2006.

How about an investment in U.S. Savings bonds? A $1,000 investment will mature at $2,000 in 7 years, which equals about $142 in simple interest each year. Americans are currently experiencing around 3-5% inflation (with significantly higher numbers foecast), which means the purchasing power of your $1,000 deteriorates by about $45 per year.

Aside from inflation, wealth-builders must be aware of tax the implications inherent to any business success.

Taxes are a way of life, and are essential to maintain a stable government. During the year 2003, 19.7 million tax returns were filed for non-farm, sole proprietorship enterprises. Taxes paid from this group equaled more than 230 billion dollars.

Of around 88.8 million returns filed with taxes due annually, the average income tax payable is over $8,412. It is unclear from the IRS tax tables if this includes total federal income tax paid, or just the amount the average filer paid to make up any balance due to the federal government.

One thing is certain, however, these figures do not include state and local taxes, property taxes, and sales taxes paid by the individual consumer.

Millionaire Secret #14
Buy Appreciable Assets

It's probably obvious to you that investments must appreciate in order to build wealth.

However, how much of your expendable income goes for appreciable assets versus depreciable goods? Do you find yourself at the end of your money before the end of the month?

To build wealth and ensure the proper capitalization of your business, you must first cease the expenditure of your funds on worthless goods and focus every penny you can muster into your personal war against poverty. The first battle you must win is the Battle of the Budget.

Get control of your spending, or it will control you for the rest of your life.

On a national level, America has not suffered a depression since the 1930s. On average, real estate values have increased every year for the past 70 years, with some spectacular growth noted in boom areas, such as the Southwest, and some decline in values in the industrial heartland. Recently of course, real estate values have plummeted due to the economic crisis, but in my opinion, the values will cycle back up, creating a fresh batch of millionaires across the country.

What Are Your Options?

Overall, in my opinion, real estate has consistently been a profitable investment for Americans.

Another area of growth is the stock market. Like real estate, it has noted exceptions, and some bad years. However, over the long run, the stock market, notably quality companies sold on the New York Stock Exchange, have seen consistent growth above inflation rates for the past 70 years.

Antique furniture, automobiles, art, and jewelry also see consistent gains in value, while contemporary furniture, automobiles, and jewelry typically loses value immediately after its purchase.

For example, if you purchase a new car, the moment you drive it off the dealer's lot, it becomes worth significantly less than the payoff for the loan you just signed. Likewise, if you purchase a brand new couch, and choose to resell it, the resale value will be a fraction of your initial purchase price.

The Essence Of Creating Wealth

The essence of creating wealth is to restrict your expenditure of scarce financial resources on depreciable consumer goods, and direct those same resources towards the purchase of items that appreciate in value and possibly throw off positive cash flow.

One investment that is often overlooked is education.

I'm not necessarily talking about college, although a college education can give you a solid foundation to build upon. The education I'm referring to is the focused training you can receive that is directly pertinent to your area of interest--such as sales, investments, business management, collectibles, etc.

This training can come in the form of books, tapes, seminars, or hands-on experience. As an alternative to buying tapes (remember, we want to minimize spending where possible), consider visiting your community library.

Check out some of the tapes produced by the Nightingale organization and start listening to them during your commutes.

Here is a short list of the most popular wealth and success oriented tapes selling on Amazon:

Seven Habits of Highly Effective People, Stephen Covey
Think and Grow Rich, Napoleon Hill
The Power of Positive Thinking, Norman Vincent Peale
NLP: The New Technology of Achievement, Charles Faulkner
Multiple Streams of Income, Robert Allen
The Psychology of Achievement, Brian Tracy
5 Steps to Successful Selling, Zig Ziglar
Lead the Field, Earl Nightingale

To achieve personal wealth, you must learn to acquire appreciable assets.

Thus, your fourteenth step to wealth is to forego the purchase of depreciable assets and focus all of your resources on acquiring income producing assets that typically appreciate in value, rather than depreciate.

"The key to creating wealth is to you're your cash assets into businesses and investments that provide positive cash flow to you for the foreseeable future.

Once your passive income has exceeded your living expenses, you have achieved an entry level of wealth and have laid the foundation for exponential growth."

The Millionaire's Secret

Millionaire Secret #15
The Power and Risks of Leverage

Leverage is a powerful tool that significantly increases your purchasing and investment power.

Used properly, leverage can propel you into wealth. Used improperly, it can send you to bankruptcy court post haste. Therefore, your fifteenth step towards creating wealth is to master the art of using leverage.

Consider this example. A home in your neighborhood is for sale and the price is $100,000. It looks like a good investment so you buy it. In situation one you pay cash for the home: total investment $100,000. In situation two you put $10,000 down on the house and finance the remaining $90,000.

At the end of the year inflation and some improvements you've made to the property have increased its value to $110,000, a 10% rate of appreciation. In situation one, your $100,000 investment has increased by 10%. In situation two, your $10,000 investment has increased by 100%. This is the power of leverage.

If you had $100,000 to invest, which would you prefer, a 10% return or a 100% return? Real estate empires are built on the power of leverage.

Understanding Your Capital Base

A vitally important concept in the use of leverage is to never touch your capital base. Your capital base is the financial and human resources you have available for investment.

There is a story of a small New England town made up of "old" wealth residents. Old wealth is wealth held by generations of families, passed from parent to child, over and over.

A visitor noted that the other residents ignored a certain man. When the man walked down the street mothers would grab their children and race to the other side, just to avoid coming in contact with this man.

The visitor was perplexed and asked a passerby what crime this man had committed. The answer: "He dipped into his capital base."

In other words, he had spent part of the money that his forefathers had set aside for investment purposes. Whenever you "dip into your capital base" you are effectively destroying your wealth building, and wealth sustaining, capability.

Dipping into your capital base is the cardinal sin of investment and empire building.

The lesson of building and preserving your capital base cannot be over emphasized. Please, take this wealth building strategy seriously. In fact, I highly recommend you read (or re-read, as the case may be) George Clason's book, "The Richest Man in Babylon" just to reinforce the concept of building and preserving your capital base.

A Personal Story About Protecting Your Capital Base

My grandmother had two pecan trees in her backyard. I can remember as a child picking up bags of pecans from her lawn and setting on her back porch eating pecans as fast as I could shell them.

Those trees stood for nearly one hundred years before being destroyed by a tornado, but while they stood they provided shade during the hot summer afternoons, and a source of food, beauty, and joy almost year around.

As a child she and her sister were each given two pecans from a visitor to their home. My great aunt reportedly ate her pecans immediately, but my grandmother planted her pecans in the backyard, and then nurtured the seedlings until they became trees.

Planting and nurturing the seeds of your capital base will provide for you and your grandchildren. Don't let the opportunity to create wealth for your posterity go to waste by eating, rather than planting, the seeds of wealth.

"Think long and hard before dipping you're your capital base.

Remember, when you spend your capital base on depreciable assets or consumer goods, you are effectively "eating" the seeds of your future."

The Millionaire's Secret

Millionaire Secret #16
Focus Your Efforts In Areas Where You Excel

We've all been told a hundred times not to put all our eggs in one basket.

This is a perfect example of the baloney financial losers feed to people around them.

Look at any wealthy man and you will see a history of concentrated effort in one area. Sure, they may be diversified now, but when they were building their wealth, you can bet everything they had was locked into one thing.

Examples include Sam Walton of Wal-Mart, Bill Gates of Microsoft, and Michael Dell of Dell Computers. These men may be diversified now (sadly, Sam Walton has passed), but when they were building their enterprises, every ounce of effort and coin in their pocket was dedicated to that business.

Andrew Carnegie once stated, "put all your eggs in one basket, then watch that basket very well." The point is, you need to focus your efforts, and most importantly, you need to pay attention to what you are doing.

Master the fundamentals of the business or investment of your choice. Know the ins and outs of your industry like a professional, and concentrate your resources in this area. With your expertise in a given area, you can aggressively seek opportunities other people may not even be aware of.

Stepping Outside Your Comfort Zone

Lofty dreams may require you to step outside your comfort zone, but true opportunities are rarely easily had. Consider the founder of the Hilton hotel conglomerate.

Conrad Hilton was born and raised in a small town in New Mexico, which you may think is hardly the background for an international hotel magnate. Early in his career as he struggled to find himself, his mother told him: "Conrad, if you want to launch big ships, you have to go where the water is deep."

He left New Mexico and threw himself into the shark-infested waters of a Texas oil town. If he had stayed home he would probably have led a happy, somewhat successful life in New Mexico. But he chose otherwise and headed for deeper waters.

Similarly, if you have big plans and lofty dreams, you'll have to put yourself in the environment capable of supporting those goals. Not too many people become millionaires selling fishing worms on the street corner, but a chain of bait shops might do the trick.

Also, the idea of dealing with tenants and property management may not appeal to you, but if you want to build a real estate fortune you'll have to immerse yourself in it.

The point is, you must be aggressive and seek out opportunity. You may have to change your lifestyle and/or your habits to do this, but change is inherent to growth.

Therefore, your sixteenth step towards wealth is to master a narrow market niche and exploit it in an ethical and legal manner to maximize your wealth creation.

"Creating wealth may require you to step outside your comfort zone.

While others are spending the weekend water skiing, or vacationing in Hawaii, you will be working overtime to build a business or locate rental properties.

As Dave Ramsey often states, "You have to live like nobody else, so that one day you can live like nobody else." It may not always be fun, but that is what it takes to create wealth."

The Millionaire's Secret

Millionaire Secret #17
Invest for Long-Term Growth

Entrepreneurs and beginning investors must be aggressive, but you don't have to be careless or foolish.

Concentrate your investments in markets where you know and accept the associated risks. For example, if you invest in the futures market, you must be prepared to lose your entire nest egg in a heartbeat. However, this can also be an area of fantastic returns on your investment.

Other investments, like savings accounts, may offer safety, but offer little in the way of appreciation. Your task is to find the investments and business opportunities which offer a level of risk you can live with, while rewarding you sufficiently to reach your wealth building goals.

Some investments, which offer stability and growth, include real estate, numismatic coins, and antiques.

Your Best Investment Choice...

In my opinion, however, the best investment in the world is a small business that you own and operate. Read books on small business management, attend seminars sponsored by the Small Business Administration, and talk to other small business owners.

One source of information that people think is great is the college; however, I have a problem taking business advice from a teacher who teaches about business but has probably never operated his or her own profitable business.

The classroom is a great place to learn about the theory of business and investing, but search for your mentors beyond the classroom. Wealth builders must learn from the school of hard knocks, and without the valuable experience gained from your daily exposure to the marketplace, and observation of other successful people, you will never learn to succeed or control your investments.

A wealth builder assumes responsibility for his wealth program and does not abdicate control of his resources to anyone. Absentee ownership is fine for the wealthy, but the wealth builder needs to be on hand.

Nobody in the world cares about your future as much as you do, and nobody cares about your assets as much as you do.

If you want to get ahead, maintain control of your budding empire. Watch your assets like a mother hen watches her chicks. However, with all this effort to build wealth, don't lose sight of the big picture. In all your getting, don't lose sight of who you are, and don't forsake the love of family and friends.

Entrepreneurs are driven to succeed by an uncontrollable urge to surpass those around them. They are willing to work atrocious hours, sacrifice leisure, forego vacations, and focus every waking minute of their attention to their baby venture.

This is fine for some people, but most of us need to take time to maintain relationships and rest the body and soul. Don't sweat the time spent with your family. And don't ignore your body's demands for rest.

You Will Become A Wealth Magnet

As your wealth increases, you will be bombarded by offers from friends, relatives, and strangers for help with their projects. Invariably this will entail your taking the financial risks while they enjoy the benefits of success.

Shy away from other people's projects. Focus on what got you where you are. In his excellent book "In Search of Excellence," Tom Peters advised business owners to "stick to their knitting." That is, do what you are good at, and nothing else.

For friends and relatives you wish to help, help them by teaching them the Millionaire's Secret.

Therefore, the seventeenth step in your creating wealth journey is to protect your assets, focus on what you are good at, and continue to build your wealth through wise investments.

Conclusion
Houston, We Have a Problem

According to the Social Security Administration, over 95% of us will never achieve our financial dreams.

Sadly, most of us will never even clear the launch tower.

But take heart. In my experience the odds are more in your favor than you may believe. Consider that out of 100 people, at least half of them are content with living lives of "quiet desperation," and make no effort to change what they perceive as their "lot in life."

Of the remaining 50, many of them have dreams and goals that do not include seeking wealth. For example, I have neighbors who work regular jobs and live for the weekend. They are solid, hard working people, and I'm happy to have them as friends, neighbors, and co-workers.

So, while my numbers are pure estimates, in my opinion only 10 people out of every hundred are interested in creating wealth. And out of those 10 wealth builders, only a handful will actually take deliberate action to make something happen.

The Social Security Administration's facts are accurate in this area. Only 5% of us achieve financial independence at retirement. But so what, as active wealth builders, we are in a select group where the odds of success are significantly in our favor. You can improve the odds even further by following a few simple rules:

1. Learn to spend less than you earn.
2. Invest your expendable cash into appreciable assets.
3. Protect your assets and continually strive to create sources of passive income.
4. Never touch your capital base.

If you can study and follow these simple rules, you will shouting, "Houston, we have cleared the tower."

Wealth And the School Of Hard Knocks

I like to take a no-holds-barred approach to business.

That means when I see an opportunity, and decide it offers a low risk and high payoff potential, I jump in.

I've been burned a few times in my over-zealousness, but an occasional failure is part of the game. Over the years I've learned that you either play the game, and accept the risks (it helps to understand the risks going in), or you don't play.

In my opinion, life is too short to waste time on the sidelines. I rode the bench in high school football and hated every minute of it. The publication you now hold is an expression of my "play the game" business philosophy.

So please, be a player, not a spectator.

I hold a masters degree in business administration, and have worked in public and private industry for over 25 years. But don't let that throw you off your game plan.

Most of what I've learned about business I learned on the streets, playing the game, getting knocked down a few times, and getting back up in time for the next play.

During the past 12 years I have built and managed several successful companies using a technique of (1) educating myself about a business opportunity, (2) diving in and learning from hands-on experience, and (3) using this knowledge and new found experience to gain insight into how to play the game better, and how to adapt my behavior to find either a profit in the business, or minimize my losses.

Throughout the trials and joys of business ownership, I have learned there is one constant in life: nothing stays the same.

Change is everywhere.

Be flexible. Treat every circumstance as a learning opportunity, and never rest on yesterday's successes; for tomorrow is another day.

In the end, don't let the words "he/she had the potential to achieve great things" be a part of your epitaph.

The words "had" and "potential" are clues to a life full of promise never realized. Woody Allen once said, "eighty percent of success is showing up." You have to show up.

You have to be willing to take the plunge. You have to do the things other people refuse to do. You have to persevere in the face of adversity. And, you have to believe in yourself, no matter what others may say and think about you.

Fortunately, there are literally hundreds of opportunities out there, waiting for you.

You've taken the first step towards a brighter future for yourself and your family by reading this book.

Thanks for your trust. Hold nothing back. Take no prisoners. Enter the game and remove yourself from the "gray twilight" of neither victory nor defeat.

The worse that can happen is that you will learn a lot about running a business, and more about human nature. The best that can happen will depend upon you. In today's world, you truly set the limits to your success.

Keep Reading

Finally, it has been said that leaders are readers.

I sincerely believe wealth-builders are leaders, and rightly so, as building an empire takes networking with other people. Are you a reader?

How many non-fiction books have you read this year? If you have read more than 5, you are far above the average, but short of the aggressive leader level. I suggest you read at least one non-fiction book per month in your field of interest or business endeavor.

Go ahead and buy that discount card from your Barnes and Noble dealer — you're going to need it.

Success in life and business is about learning how to play the game, getting involved, and never quitting.

The Millionaire's Secret